77 SECRETS
to Leadership Success

by
Kathy Larsen

Beaver's Pond Press

To order additional copies contact:
The Training Center®
(402) 334-9414 • FAX (402) 331-4709
P.O. Box 45526
Omaha, NE 68145-0526

Milton Adams – Production Coordinator
Mark LeBlanc – Marketing Resource

Dedicated to

My husband Don for his support, encouragement,
and incredible belief in me.

My daughter Amanda for always being such an inspiration
to me and for seeing me as a special leader in her life.

My step daughter Carey for helping me think about things differently.

My step son Corey for showing me how easy it can be
to realize a dream.

As you apply these simple yet **powerful** Secrets to Leadership Success… happiness and prosperity will happen in your life and in the lives of those around you.

Create a vision and mission for your company, organization, department. Get input from people on your team!

Identify expectations clearly and hold people accountable for them.

Make yourself available. No matter what level you are in the organization.

Over-communicate what is going on in the organization.

Involve your people in problem solving at every level of the company.

Listen, Listen Listen to your customers/clients and employees then Act on what you hear.

Hold regular "Town Hall" meetings where two way communication is encouraged!

Embrace change with energy and enthusiasm. Involve people at all levels to provide ideas and take responsibility for positive change.

Reward Risk Takers.

Take the learning from failures and reward it!

Be empathic and understanding of people's feelings as they work through major changes.

Understand that people are different and treat them as they want to be treated. It may not be the same for everyone.

See more in people than they see in themselves. It stimulates growth.

Smile...it's contagious!

Manage the progress of your company/ department goals by changing them as needed. Nothing is set in stone.

Treat people as team players not subordinates.

Understand and adjust to people's needs as a person.

Motivate by mission versus motivate by fear. It works!

See problems as opportunities and encourage that in your people.

Help people *discover* their strengths and areas to strengthen.

Value people for who they are, what they do, and how they contribute to your organization's success.

Help people *discover* what to do instead of *telling* them what to do. They will be more inclined to do it if it's their idea.

Really empower people to take responsibility and accountability.

Involve your people in problem solving and decision making as much as possible. You will be encouraged by the positive solutions and amazed at the commitment to move forward.

Make sure *everyone* shares their input, not just the people who come forward. Ask them often, give them time to respond, then act on what they say.

Teach people to be change agents and reward them for it.

Help *everyone* realize their value in exceeding customer/client and co-worker expectations… no matter what job they perform.

Create an environment where it is okay to challenge policies and procedures or the status quo.

Develop compensation based 50% on what they do (results) and 50% on how they do it.

Make tough decisions when necessary and communicate them quickly to *everyone* who is affected by them.

Believe in people, have confidence in them, and give them plenty of positive reinforcement.

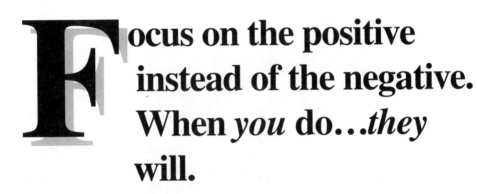

Focus on the positive instead of the negative. When *you* do...*they* will.

Reward people every day in many creative ways.

Remember little things mean everything.

Give specific, Positive, Encouraging, Caring and Sincere feedback to people every day (SPECS©).

36

Acknowledge everyone at every level in a personal way.

Demonstrate a positive attitude at all times about your job, the direction of your organization, and every level of management. Attitude is everything!

Remember when you point your finger, three fingers are pointing back at you.

Maintain optimism and confidence in the direction of your organization always.

Demonstrate consistency in your personal behavior and your relations with people.

Demonstrate a genuine care and concern for people in your daily activities. They will notice it and pass it on to others.

Create informal and formal feedback mechanisms for employees and customers.

Create a strong open line of communications. Secrets create negative feelings and low productivity. Create an atmosphere where there are no secrets!

Be energetic and enthusiastic in all that you do.

**F**ocus direction and decisions on values and ethics.

Be sensitive to people and goal driven at the same time.

Have a balance in your life that people see on a regular basis.

Inspire people to be who and what they want to be. Productivity will soar!

Accept people where they are, but view them as they can become. It's very rewarding!

Create a foundation and let the people build the business.

Really walk your talk—(Ask people how you are doing...then listen *non-defensively*).

Really respect and value your people at all levels. The test is "do they feel valued and respect-ed?" ASK THEM!

Guide people toward individual and team goals.

Give *more* information. If you think you have given enough… give more…then give more.

Appreciate people for what they do for your organization.

56

Help people with personal situations if necessary.

Encourage creativity in people at all levels and reward it.

Ensure that everyone knows, understands, and enrolls in the mission and purpose of your company, organization or department.

Be a positive mentor. People *want* to learn from you.

Hire people who are different than you.

Create diversity in your company and on your teams.

Be flexible. Flexibility is the lifeblood of an organization.

Remove barriers and roadblocks for people.

Provide training that creates behavior change in people.

Remember that success on the job depends much more on feelings, attitudes, and emotions than knowledge, skills, and abilities.

Catch people doing things right…often! Share it verbally or put it in writing.

Use open ended who, what, where, why, when, how, tell me about, describe for me questions to get people talking and you *listening*.

Develop leaders at all levels of your organization.

Remember you can't motivate people, you can only create an environment where people want to be motivated.

About 77% of what is seen, heard, and read daily is negative. It takes a concentrated effort to focus on the positive.

Have fun and encourage fun in the workplace. It creates an environment where people *want* to come to work.

Remember as you value and respect your employees they will value and respect you and each other. As they value and respect each other, the customers/clients are valued and respected. As your customers/clients are valued and respected they will provide repeat business and referrals for new business. This effects the bottom line of your organization. IT STARTS WITH YOU!

Get out among your employees regularly and talk to them as people. SMILE!

Trust people! It relieves stress and enhances productivity.

Have a "Can DO" Attitude!

Radiate the attitude of well being, confi-dence and enthusi-asm—others will follow your lead.

Remember: A leader is someone people *want* to follow!

The following pages are for your personal use. I recommend that you select up to three Leadership Secrets to apply each week to help you become the type of leader people *want* to follow. Remember…it takes 21-32 days to create a behavior change.

I will apply the following Leadership Success Secrets every day this week:

_____

_____

_____

_____

_____

_____

_____

_____

Name: _____

Date: _____

I will apply the following Leadership Success Secrets every day this week:

_____

_____

_____

_____

_____

_____

_____

_____

_____

Name: _____

Date: _____

I will apply the following Leadership Success Secrets every day this week:

_____

_____

_____

_____

_____

_____

_____

_____

Name: _____

Date: _____

I will apply the following Leadership Success Secrets every day this week:

_____

_____

_____

_____

_____

_____

_____

_____

Name: _____

Date: _____

About the Author...

Kathy Larsen works with companies who want to grow their business and leaders who want to create a positive work environment. She conducts presentations and workshops around the country on a variety of topics about how to value people and take responsibility for results.

Her company, The Training Center®, provides programs and educational materials designed to incorporate value focused principles into the work environment. Kathy is a successful corporate leader, entrepreneur, consultant, speaker, and business owner. Hundreds of clients have relied on her experience and expertise in the areas of Customer/Employee Satisfaction, Sales, and Leadership.

Value Focused Leadership Principles

are necessary for successful businesses, prosperous communities, and happy families. This book provides a great gift for people at all levels.

If you would like to learn more about volume discounts, want to share your own Secrets to Leadership Success, or need more information about books, seminars and presentations please contact:

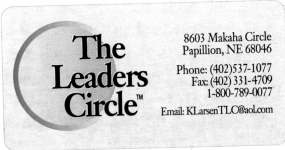

The Leaders Circle™

8603 Makaha Circle
Papillion, NE 68046

Phone: (402)537-1077
Fax: (402) 331-4709
1-800-789-0077

Email: KLarsenTLC@aol.com